Emperor Qin's Terra Cotta Army

UNEARTHING ANCIENT WORLDS

Michael Capek

Twenty-First Century Books · Minneapolis

For Terri

The author gratefully acknowledges the contribution of Dr. Kristin Stapleton, Director of Asian Studies, University of Buffalo, New York.

Twenty-First Century Books
A division of Lerner Publishing Group, Inc.
241 First Avenue North
Minneapolis, MN 55401 U.S.A.

Website address: www.lernerbooks.com

Library of Congress Cataloging-in-Publication Data

Capek, Michael.
    Emperor Qin's terra cotta army / by Michael Capek.
        p.   cm. — (Unearthing Ancient Worlds)
    Includes bibliographical references and index.
    ISBN 978-0-8225-7507-8 (lib. bdg. : alk. paper)
    1. Qin shi huang, Emperor of China, 259–210 B.C.—Tomb. 2. Terra-cotta sculpture, Chinese—Qin-Han dynasties, 221 B.C.–220 A.D. 3. Shaanxi Sheng (China)—Antiquities. I. Title.
DS747.9.C47C37 2008
931'.04—dc22   2007025002

Manufactured in the United States of America
1 2 3 4 5 6 – PA – 13 12 11 10 09 08

TABLE OF CONTENTS

The burial mound of China's first emperor, Qin Shi Huangdi (259 B.C.–210 B.C.) rises from

INTRODUCTION

For centuries, farmers living in villages east of Xi'an in northwestern China heard stories of ghosts and spirits living beneath the earth. Everyone knew that many years ago, this area had been the home of China's earliest emperors. Many people believed that their restless spirits still lurked about, eager for mischief—or worse.

The first emperor of China was Qin Shi Huangdi. The ruins of his ancient palace lay on the Wei River not far away. His burial mound overlooked the surrounding fields. Generations of farmers had plowed and harvested this land. Some people climbed the mound's steep sides to see the view from the top. But most locals were far too busy to think much about what might lie buried under the mound—or under the wide, flat fields around it.

Over the years, people had found objects buried in these fields. Farmers had stumbled over small statues. Their hoes had hit oddly marked bits of pottery and stone. Some superstitious people avoided the fields altogether.

One old tale told of a farmer in the early twentieth century. He was digging in a field near the ancient emperor's tomb. The earth suddenly crumbled beneath his feet, revealing an underground cave. Standing there looking at him was the perfectly formed, life-sized figure of a man—a man made entirely

This illustration of Qin Shi Huangdi is from an album of Chinese emperors from the 1700s.

of stone. The farmer was terrified, thinking it must be an evil spirit. He smashed the figure to pieces with his shovel and filled up the hole.

Years passed. They were stormy ones for China. Modern wars and a major revolution brought social and political change. But farmers still worked the fields surrounding the First Emperor's tomb as they had for centuries. Life in rural China was difficult. Growing food for hungry people always seemed more important than broken pieces of pottery in the plowed ground.

FAST FACTS ABOUT EMPEROR QIN'S TERRA COTTA ARMY

- The terra cotta army dates back to the 200s B.C.

- Emperor Qin Shi Huangdi was born as Prince Zheng of Qin in 259 B.C. The young prince was born into a world of war. For more than 250 years, Qin and six other kingdoms had been fighting for domination and control. These seven Warring States made up much of what later became modern China.

- Prince Zheng became king when he was thirteen years old. As he grew older, he changed from an inexperienced young prince to a decisive warrior king. He created one of the world's most powerful armies. His forces went on to defeat the other Warring States. Zheng became Qin Shi Huangdi, the first emperor of a unified Chinese empire.

- Qin Shi Huangdi's terra cotta army was probably meant to protect the emperor in the afterlife. It was buried in pits near the emperor's tomb after his death in 210 B.C.

- A group of Chinese farmers discovered a few figures of this huge army in 1974

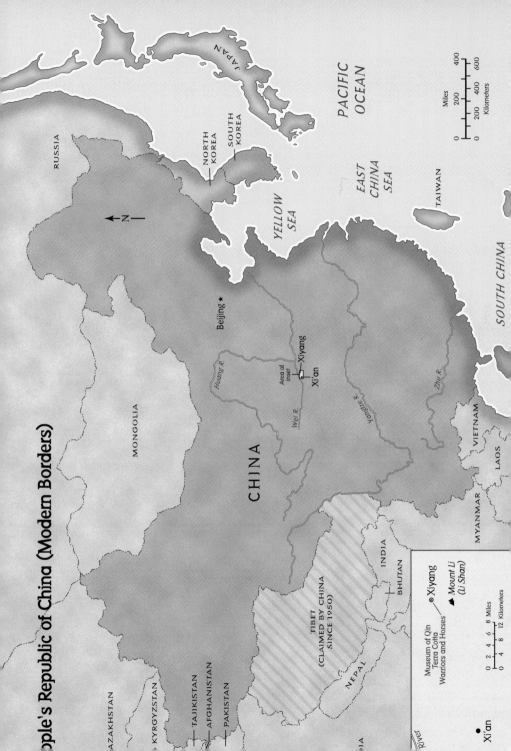

People's Republic of China (Modern Borders)

RUSSIA

KAZAKHSTAN

KYRGYZSTAN

TAJIKISTAN

AFGHANISTAN

PAKISTAN

MONGOLIA

CHINA

TIBET
(CLAIMED BY CHINA
SINCE 1950)

NEPAL

BHUTAN

INDIA

MYANMAR

LAOS

VIETNAM

NORTH KOREA

SOUTH KOREA

JAPAN

TAIWAN

YELLOW SEA

EAST CHINA SEA

PACIFIC OCEAN

SOUTH CHINA

Beijing ★

Huang R.

Wei R.

Yangtze R.

Zhu R.

Xiyang

Xi'an

Area of inset

N

Museum of Qin
Terra Cotta
Warriors and Horses

⊚ Xiyang

▲ Mount Li
(Li Shan)

• Xi'an

0   2   4   6   8 Miles
0   4   8   12 Kilometers

0   200   400
Miles

0   200   400   600
Kilometers

CHAPTER one

AN ACCIDENTAL DISCOVERY

The morning of March 29, 1974, is cool. Six farmers from the village of Xiyang, in Lintong County, arrive at a dusty field. The area lies about 1 mile (1.6 kilometers) east of the First Emperor's tomb mound. Northwestern China has suffered from a drought (a long period without rain), and the village needs water. Without it, growing crops will be nearly impossible. The farmers carry picks and shovels. They plan to dig a well.

The men walk a few steps off the dirt road and begin to dig. The ground is as hard as concrete. It takes the men several days to dig down 5 feet (1.5 meters). The deeper they dig, though, the easier it gets. By the time the hole is 6.5 feet (2 m) deep, the dirt is softer. The farmers' fathers and grandfathers worked this field, so they know what to expect. They are not surprised to find pieces of pottery, such as the baked red tiles used on local roofs. They move the pieces aside and dig on. If there is any water here, they should find it soon.

One day at about noon, two farmers are working at the bottom of the well. The hole is

Yang Zhifa was one of the farmers who originally discovered the terra cotta soldiers.

13 feet (4 m) deep and nearly 10 feet (3 m) wide at the top. But it is still dry. Suddenly, a shovel strikes something hard.

"At first I thought I had hit a brick," one of the men said later. "But when I scraped away the dirt, it was the length of a full body."

The man drops his shovel and kneels in the bottom of the hole. He brushes away the dirt. He doesn't find a brick or a rock. He glimpses something round and oddly colored. He continues clearing around the object.

A form emerges—the form of a human body! Not a real person but part of a beautifully made statue. It is made of baked clay called terra cotta. Two of the men dig around the curved piece until they free it. The farmers look around the bottom of the hole. They see more pieces of pottery scattered about. They also see bits of stone and metal. One man picks up a perfect bronze arrowhead. It gleams in the light from above. The tip is as sharp as if it had just been made. Other pieces of twisted metal gleam in the dim light. And the men see a face staring up at them—a perfectly formed terra cotta head.

Excitedly, the men call to their friends who are resting above. They pass several pottery pieces and metal fragments up to them. In the bright glare of day, the men stare at the relics in silence. They are amazed to see such large and beautiful terra cotta. It has clearly been shaped and marked by human hands.

One of the men backs away, frowning. He does not even want to look at the things. He thinks they might be evil. They should be reburied immediately, he says. The men who found the pieces climb out of the hole. One of them reminds the others of a meeting a few months ago. The government's Cultural Relics Bureau had held the meeting. At that meeting, an archaeologist from the city told the local people about this region's fascinating history.

Chinese archaeologists found this bronze arrowhead buried with the terra cotta army in the early 1980s.

Law of the Land

The government oversees most aspects of people's lives in modern China. A government office or group is in charge of nearly everything. For example, before anyone can dig or explore in China, they must get permission from the area's Cultural Relics Bureau. This modern system has its beginnings during the Qin dynasty (221-206 B.C.) (A dynasty is a line of rulers who are all from the same family.) Archaeologists have found more than one thousand pieces of bamboo in Shuihudi, and thousands more in other parts of China. The pieces are covered with records written during that period. They have shed new light on social, political, military, and economic aspects of life during the Qin dynasty.

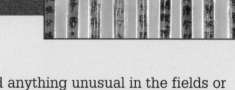

These bamboo slips found in the Chinese city of Shuihudi are records of the Qin dynasty.

He also told them that if they ever found anything unusual in the fields or streams of Lintong County, they must report it immediately.

The men finally agree that they should show their discovery to someone. They carefully place several of the pieces in a three-wheeled cart. Together they roll it to the village of Xiyang, about 1 mile (1.6 km) away.

The next day, an archaeologist arrives from Xi'an. Xi'an is a large city 40 miles (64 km) to the west. The archaeologist examines the pottery pieces and questions the farmers. He grows excited and hurries to phone the district Cultural Relics Bureau. The bureau gives him permission to drill some holes in the field. These test holes reveal a huge amount of pottery and other material under the ground. These things are not just near the well but all over the field. Almost every place the archaeologist drills, he finds hints of ancient artifacts. His report a few days later is almost beyond belief. A full-scale excavation of the site is necessary, he urges. China's top archaeologists should come to survey the area as soon as possible.

Workers at the dig carefully tag each piece of terra cotta so that they can keep track of where each piece came from. The pieces will be assembled in nearby sheds.

CHAPTER two

A SPIRIT CITY

On July 17, 1974, a group meets at the field near Xiyang. The team includes experts from the Cultural Relics Bureau and archaeologists from universities all over China. The farmers who made the first discovery are nearby. They are eager to answer questions or help in any way they can.

The pieces of terra cotta and metal first appeared in the Lintong grain field four months ago. Since then many archaeologists have looked at them. No one has seen anything like them before. They are even more interesting because they were so close to Qin Shi Huangdi's tomb.

The team agrees with the district archaeologist. Experts should examine the entire area around the well. They will excavate it—carefully dig it up. A team made up of archaeologists from several colleges and science institutes in Shaanxi Province will guide the excavation.

TRACKING DOWN TREASURES

The team sets up a headquarters at Xiyang. Dr. Yuan Zhongyi is one of the team leaders. He is also an archaeology teacher. Yuan pitches a tent in the middle of the grain field. He tells everyone that he plans to stay here for a week or two, while the team studies the site. Then he will go back to teaching at the university in Xi'an.

Yuan hears that local people have been coming to the field. Some of them have taken away pieces of pottery and other items. But the archaeologists need to study every piece. He politely visits homes and takes back items. One of them is an extremely lifelike pottery head. Yuan finds it perched on the mantel over the fireplace in an old woman's home. She thought it was the face of an ancient god. She hoped that it would bring good luck into her house.

The mid-July sun beats down on the team of archaeologists. They begin to dig holes in the dry field. Local farmers and students help them. They start at the well the farmers dug earlier. Workers use probes—sharp, drill-like tools on long poles—to find out what is under the ground. They move outward, going north and south from the well.

The probes take samples of earth 10 to 15 feet (3 to 5 m) beneath the surface. The workers are surprised to find red, scorched earth and the

City of Spirits

The mound over the emperor's burial chamber lies in the southern part of a much bigger rectangle. Originally, high walls and a water-filled moat surrounded the whole area. Even after two thousand years, the mound still stands 141 feet (43 m) high. It covers more than 12,000 square feet (1,115 sq. m). Huge inner and outer earth walls surround the burial area. Ancient workers made these cementlike walls by packing down many layers of damp dirt. The remains of these strong walls still exist underground. Archaeologists use probes to find them. Their tests also locate buried gates, ramps, and other features. An inner rectangular wall measures 2,116 by 1,132 feet (645 by 345 m) long. It averages 33 feet (10 m) wide at the bottom. The outer wall is 7,130 by 3,196 feet (2,173 by 974 m) long and 23 feet (7 m) wide at its base.

Some experts call this huge area "a city," though no living person has ever called it home. It was built for the spirits of the dead emperor and his servants, including his army—a "spirit city."

After archaeologists opened Pit 1, they still had a lot of work ahead of them. They needed to piece together hundreds of pieces of metal and terra cotta. This photograph was taken in 1975.

remains of charred wooden beams. These discoveries tell them that a great fire once burned a huge structure here. Pieces of pottery, bronze arrow points, and other unusual items begin coming up as well. The digging also reveals an eastern wall or foundation of a building. It is made of hard-packed earth. After a month of probing, the workers outline a pit about 55 feet (17 m) long and 26 feet (8 m) wide.

It seems that a vast room lies beneath the whole field. Terra cotta pottery and metallic weapons fill the chamber. Yuan and the other archaeologists are overwhelmed. No one has found anything of this sort in China before. For that matter, no one has found anything like this anyplace else in the world.

Beginning at the eastern edge of the pit, workers begin removing layers of dirt. They use picks and shovels, and they work slowly and carefully.

They scoop up more than 3,000 square feet (279 sq. m) of earth. Archaeologists sift the soil and examine every bit of metal, stone, and pottery. They carefully record everything and save it in plastic bags to study later. Trucks haul away the rest of the dirt.

At a depth of around 8 to 10 feet (2 to 3 m), the archaeologists begin finding much larger pieces of terra cotta. They discover life-sized statues—ancient terra cotta warriors. Shovels unearth arms, hands, legs, feet, and bodies made of the hard clay. Dozens of faces begin to emerge. Amazingly, they all appear to be different. Each warrior wears clothing and armor that look unique to him.

Each face has its own expression. Some warriors look serious and determined. Others seem slightly amused, puzzled, surprised, or sad. The soldiers' clay moustaches, beards, and hairstyles all seem different too. There are simple buns that seem to be held in place with pins. There are also twisted top knots made of finely woven braids. Some of the warriors wear caps or helmets. It's an incredible variety of sculpture. It is almost as if each soldier had been separately formed by hand.

Are these individual portraits of real soldiers who served during ancient times? It's too early for the archaeologists to tell. More and more figures keep coming out of the ground. The members of the team have little

Qin Craft

The Chinese already had a long terra cotta tradition before they created Emperor Qin's army. For centuries, factories throughout China had made roofing tiles, bricks, pots, and other items.

Making terra cotta began by sifting and washing clay over and over. Then workers mixed the fine, wet clay with a small amount of white quartz. Workers gathered this hard mineral on Mount Li, along with the clay. They pounded the quartz into dust and added it to the clay. They squeezed and worked the clay and quartz mixture until it was smooth. It was perfect for molding and shaping into objects. Finally, workers baked the objects at temperatures between 1,500 to 1,800°F (816 to 982°C). The result was hard, glassy terra cotta. This pottery was waterproof and easy to paint. Modern terra cotta is still made this way.

Yuan Zhongyi was one of the first archaeologists to visit the site of the terra cotta army. He later became the head of the excavation.

"Many of us had been in archaeological work for several decades and had never seen such big pottery figures or such a large pit. We still didn't believe it. After surveying the test area and making many borings, we determined that this indeed was a real find. We were jubilant!"

—Yuan Zhongyi, 1984

time to stop and wonder. First, they must find out exactly how large this chamber of warriors is. The digging must continue. A careful study of the amazing figures will have to wait.

DELICATE DISCOVERIES

Soon the workers switch from using picks and shovels to using trowels—small hand tools with flat blades and soft brushes. They gently clear away the dust and dirt of centuries. They use sticks and slivers of bamboo to get dirt out of the tiniest areas. Archaeologists take photographs and make detailed drawings of each find. They also record the finds in writing. This takes a great deal of time, but it is very important. The figures are smashed and broken, but many of the pieces are quite large. The terra cotta pieces lie in heaps where they once fell. Many edges seem to fit back together with amazing ease. In a short time, archaeologists are able to clean and put together part of a figure. They are excited beyond words. They must force themselves to slow down and be calm.

Archaeologists take measurements of the terra cotta figures to make sure their drawings of them are accurate.

Workers collect the marked and numbered pieces in wooden boxes. They carry them to nearby storage sheds. There, teams begin gluing together sections of terra cotta warriors. But it's not as easy as it seemed. Workers are dealing with thousands of nearly identical pieces. Finding two whose edges make a perfect match is difficult. One of the many archaeologists working at the site says, "If we find one piece that fits in a day, that's a lucky day."

More and more pottery is found. The team realizes that the pit must contain hundreds of clay warriors. It might even hold thousands. And that's not all. Hundreds of pieces of metal are also scattered around. They are bronze arrow points, spear points, and other weapons that many workers have never seen before. The wooden parts of the weapons rotted away long ago. But the metal is still as sharp and shiny as it was when they were first made. Some twisted metal pieces are triggers from crossbows. This terra cotta army must have carried these weapons.

But who put this amazing army here? And why?

All evidence points to Qin Shi Huangdi, China's first emperor. Yuan and other archaeologists know about the history of Qin Shi Huangdi (also called the First Emperor). They all agree that this pit of warriors must be part of his tomb complex. They believe it makes up a spirit city. Ancient people believed the spirits of the dead would live on there, much as they had in life. The excavation's location near the royal tomb mound gives the archaeologists more clues. Maybe the army was placed here to protect the emperor after his death, just as his real army did during his life.

These ideas also give clues about the army's age. The First Emperor died in 210 B.C. If the terra cotta army was made at about that time, it would be about twenty-two hundred years old.

The Crossbow

A crossbow is a bow placed crossways on a wooden frame. The frame holds an arrow against the bow's string. A shooter pulls back the string and aims the crossbow. A trigger releases the string, shooting the arrow with great force. The Chinese military used crossbows until the end of the nineteenth century.

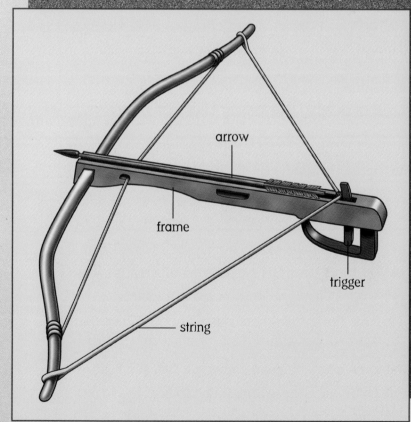

arrow

frame

trigger

string

This diagram shows a crossbow similar to those used in ancient China.

And yet no one can explain why the entire army is smashed, broken, and burned. The team finds evidence that a strong wooden roof and a layer of soil once covered the army's chamber. Workers keep finding charred wood in the soil. This wood is the remains of massive beams that once held up the roof. At some point after the army was made, the roof burned and fell. It crushed almost every clay warrior. But what started the fire? The team can't answer that question yet.

"The solid wooden construction must have been finished before the figures were put into place; otherwise their installation would have been too dangerous. At the front side of the pit, ramps have been identified down which the figures were hauled into the long, probably torch-lit corridors. This prompts an intriguing thought: nobody, not even the First Emperor, ever saw the terra cotta army in its entirety. The breathtaking view of the now world-famous columns of soldiers only became possible after excavation in 1974. Obviously, the army did not need to be seen to serve its purpose. It was enough that it was there, like inner organs concealed in a human body."

—Professor Lothar Ledderose, 1997

At the bottom of the pit, the workers find a paved floor. It is made of hundreds of bluish gray pottery bricks. Chinese characters are stamped onto every brick. Some archaeologists believe these characters are the brickmaker's name. At an ancient entrance to the room, workers also find a stone doorstep. It, too, bears the name of one of the tomb builders. Yuan points out that the First Emperor passed laws that all products in his kingdom had to bear the maker's name. People who made poor-quality goods were severely punished.

Hundreds of pottery bricks cover the pit floor where the terra cotta army stands. Many of these bricks are stamped with a maker's mark.

In the evenings, the archaeology team members gather in Yuan's tent. They go over records of the day's finds and discuss the dig. As trained scientists, archaeologists are used to finding remarkable things. But this excavation is different from anything they have ever experienced. They are like excited children. "Wouldn't it be even better if we find horses?" someone wonders. Soon everyone is saying it. "An ancient army would certainly have had horses," Yuan agrees one evening.

AN ANCIENT ANIMAL

The very next day, one of the archaeologists unearths the broken pieces of a beautiful terra cotta horse. Everyone stops their work. They gather to watch or help as the sections slowly emerge. Over several days, a full-size terra cotta horse rises out of the red soil. The statue has a wide mouth and flaring nostrils. When workers put the pieces back together, the statue will be the largest, most lifelike terra cotta horse ever found anywhere in the world. And over the next few months, workers find other horses. They uncover more than twenty in all.

Weapon Experts

Team scientists have run lab tests on the bronze sword found with the clay figures. They find that ancient workers treated the sword's blade with a coating of salt and the chemical chromium. This coating protected the metal from rust. It also made weapons nearly shatterproof, even during intense fighting. Europeans and Americans did not discover this method of preserving metal until modern times!

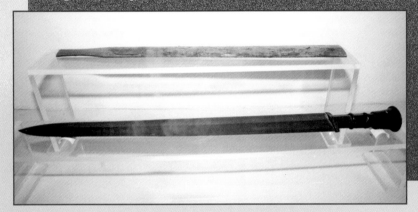

Archaeologists at the terra cotta site discovered this bronze sword still glimmering and shiny.

A few weeks after workers find the first horse, Yuan uncovers a bronze sword. Assistants number, photograph, and record it where he finds it. Then Yuan lifts the sword. He holds it almost tenderly in his gloved hands. Extraordinary! It glistens and shines in the sunlight. There is not a spot of rust on it. The edge is as sharp as it was the day it was made. Yuan says it must have been treated with some chemical. This treatment has kept the metal perfect for more than two thousand years.

The amount of terra cotta beneath the ground is almost beyond belief. In only three months, the team uncovers thousands of broken pieces of terra cotta warriors. Each one is finely detailed and seems different from the others. Arrowheads, spearheads, and other metal items also are scattered about. Workers unearth pieces of jade, gold, and bronze. Evidence continues to show that the buried warriors once held real weapons.

The archaeologists notice that many weapons appear to be missing. Some warriors' hands were clearly made to hold weapons, but those weapons are not here. It is as if someone took the bows, spears, and swords. But who might have taken them? And why would they have removed some weapons, but not others? These are more questions for scholars to think about.

"After the [Emperor's] burial had taken place someone mentioned the fact that workers and craftsmen who had constructed the mechanical devices would know about all the buried treasures and the importance of the treasures would immediately be disclosed. Consequently, when the great occasion was finished and after the treasures had been hidden away, the main entrance way to the tomb was shut off, and the outer gate lowered, so that all the workers and craftsmen who had buried the treasure were shut in, and there were none who came out again. And vegetation and trees were planted to make it look like a hill."

—historian Sima Qian, about 100 B.C.

Meanwhile, the digging has barely begun. Workers make more test holes. They show that the chamber holding the figures may cover more than 125,000 square feet (11,613 sq. m). Based on what has already been found, there must be thousands of figures here. Unbelievable! It is a true army of terra cotta soldiers!

Meanwhile, the first emperor's tomb mount looms over the excavation site, day and night. Nearly everyone working here believes these warriors are his. Surely this terra cotta army must have belonged to Qin Shi Huangdi.

Archaeologists have found hundreds of terra cotta soldiers and horses buried in the area

CHAPTER three

THE FACES OF WARRIORS

It is the summer of 1976. An army of workers and archaeologists once again descends on the pit near Qin Shi Huangdi's tomb. Yuan Zhongyi and other experts direct the team. And ancient soldiers and horses begin emerging once again. Dozens and dozens of them come out of the earth.

By now, news of the discoveries in this Chinese field has spread around the world. Experts and historians from many other countries begin arriving to see the figures. Their ideas and knowledge help the busy archaeologists. Together, they form new opinions about the meaning of the items they are finding.

GATHERING CLUES

The archaeologists notice a new and interesting fact about the warriors. Most of them were originally placed facing east. Does this have something to do with the rising sun, perhaps? No, says Yuan. The first emperor had chosen to build his capital city, Xianyang, in one of China's most protected places. High mountains rose to the west. The Wei River flowed to the south. And the Great Wall that Emperor Qin had built protected the city against invasion from the north. But the capital was open to the east. So it

Historians and experts believe the terra cotta army faced east because it was already protected by mountains in the west, the Great Wall in the north *(left)*, and the Wei River in the south *(below)*.

is likely that the emperor placed his army facing this way because he believed an attack would probably come from the east. He wanted to be ready for an invasion, even after his death.

The archaeologists put together and study more figures. It becomes clear that the soldiers are not as unique as the team thought at first. The statues' legs, arms, bodies, and heads appear to have been made in molds. Ancient workers pressed wet clay into wooden or ceramic patterns. This method sped up the work of making the figures. But before they were fired in hot kilns or ovens, each figure seems to have been carefully sculpted by hand. The faces appear to have gotten special attention. Skilled artists apparently designed each soldier's hair, moustache, and other facial features. They probably used flat wooden paddles, sharp sticks, brushes, and metal tools for this work. They also added details to the warriors' clothing and armor before baking the clay. So, while every head and body looks different, the basic parts of most soldiers are similar.

This discovery explains how the sculptors were able to create so many figures. But it does not make the terra cotta army any less amazing. The people who see and work with the warriors every day are still stunned by their find. Over time, the figures become almost like friends. One archaeologist describes the experience. He says, "Because each statue has its own personality, we have special feelings for all of them."

Looking into the warriors' faces, workers get the feeling that each figure might be an exact portrait of some member of the First Emperor's army. But why would the sculptors have gone to so much trouble? Why model thousands of different figures, only to bury them out of sight? The archaeologists and visitors at the site discuss this question for hours.

Yuan Zhongyi and others think the answer lies with the underground army's overall purpose. He believes that the emperor ordered artists to make a realistic model of his army. Then these portraits of individual warriors and servants could continue to guard him after his death.

Great Work

As the terra cotta army rises from the ground before the archaeologists' eyes, they must keep reminding themselves of one thing. The people who made these figures were simple laborers, not professional artists. A few skilled sculptors and craftsmen probably oversaw the project. But most of the workers were prisoners and slaves. Many had been sentenced to death. They would never leave this place alive. Under these terrible conditions, thousands of unhappy human beings managed to construct one of the most beautiful works of art ever seen.

As scientists, archaeologists must try to keep emotions out of their work. Still, sometimes they feel deeply moved by what ancient people accomplished here.

Clearing away the earth and dust from the figures is slow. Workers must be very careful not to damage or move any item until it's clear exactly what it is. In archaeology, the most important thing is how an object fits into the whole site. Artifacts can be precious and valuable in themselves. But it is what they mean together that gives them lasting importance. Only time will tell what this vast underground army really means, historically and artistically. Archaeologists, historians, art scholars, and scientists will study and debate that question for years to come.

Years pass. Workers excavate more and more of Pit 1, as the dig area is called. As they work, the true nature and meaning of the terra cotta army come into sharper focus.

One important finding is confusing at first. The army seems to be ceremonial, not practical. After all, it stands in a tomb, not on a battlefield. But the warriors also carry the best weapons of their day. Experts think that tens of thousands of weapons might exist in all. The hands of most warriors were clearly formed to hold actual weapons. In addition, workers find the remains of many bundles of arrows and stockpiles of other weapons in the pits. So the chambers once held large numbers of real weapons. Some of them even show evidence of actually having been used in battle. This discovery reveals that the warriors were not made to be merely a work of art. They were meant to be an actual army, armed and ready to fight.

As workers assemble more figures, they also see more of dazzling paint

Looking Deeper

After artists added details to each warrior, painters decorated the statues with different colors. This variety also makes it seem at first that each soldier is a real individual. In the same way, the horses were made of premolded parts. But workers gave them individual touches too.

An expert named Colin C. Mackenzie says, "Despite the appearance of uniqueness, the figures are probably the world's first mass-produced art." So in a way, the terra cotta army is a huge optical illusion. It is not what it appears to be at first glance.

Many of the terra cotta soldiers have hands that were formed to hold weapons. The massive army looks like it is ready for battle.

that once covered the warriors. They find traces of red, brown, blue, purple, yellow, and green on some warriors' clothing, shoes, and headgear. Workers also find traces of paint in the soil around the figures. As usual, the warriors themselves go from the pit to a shop for repair and study.

But then something terrible happens. Almost as soon as air and sunlight touch the warriors, their paint begins to peel and flake. Within minutes, the beautiful colors are gone. Only the grayish terra cotta remains. Everyone is horrified. They must do something to preserve the paint on other figures. But what? The problem is serious. It nearly brings the excavation to a halt. Many archaeologists are quite upset. They must find a way to save the paint, as well as the figures themselves.

CHAPTER four

THE SEARCH
WIDENS

Even as work in Pit 1 continues, test excavations take place in other parts of the field. The archaeologists believe that more underground chambers must be nearby. And they hope that those chambers hold other remarkable things.

Sure enough, the team receives a tip from an elderly farmer. He once worked the field next to Pit 1. His tip leads workers to another underground vault. It lies only 65 feet (20 m) north of Pit 1's eastern edge. Tests show that this new pit—called Pit 2—is L-shaped. It covers about 64,500 square feet (5,992 sq. m). Pit 2 contains vast amounts of terra cotta too. It also holds pieces of jade, gold, bone, iron, bronze, and other materials. And workers in Pit 2 find the remains of a number of horse-drawn chariots, plus many weapons. Some of these weapons have never been seen before.

STILL MORE SOLDIERS

A month later, test digging unearths a third chamber. Pit 3 is not nearly as large as the others. But it too contains pottery figures. A quick look reveals a few bronze arrowheads, one war chariot, and sixty soldiers. Nearly all of these soldiers are missing their heads.

Studies of Pit 3 reveal that these warriors are all high-ranking officers.

Their clothing and armor show that they are important. But these soldiers also stand especially tall and straight. This posture gives the team another clue that these warriors are special. Immediately, archaeologists conclude that this pit must represent the army's command center.

If the experts are right, Pit 1 must house the army's main battle formation. This group includes archers (soldiers who shoot arrows) and foot soldiers. Pit 2 seems to contain the cavalry (soldiers on horseback) and war chariots. Workers have excavated fifteen sections of Pit 2 so far. They have revealed more than two hundred terra cotta warriors, eleven wooden chariots, and nearly one hundred terra cotta horses. Many of the horses wear saddles, as if they are ready to charge into battle. The dig also reveals up to two thousand bronze weapons and weapon parts.

The number of warriors and horses in the pits is amazing. The archaeologists work nearly day and night trying to determine exactly what is here. No one has ever found such a huge number of historical relics in one place. Excitement remains high all the time.

Time is short, though. Soon China's rainy season will come, and water will flood the pits. This water could damage or destroy many valuable relics. But cleaning and removing the objects is slow and careful work. There are not enough trained workers to finish everything that needs to be done. Finally, the team decides to refill Pits 2 and 3 with earth. The soil will protect delicate objects until workers can safely excavate them. They do not fill in Pit 1, however. It's much too large. They can only try to remove as much as possible before the rains come.

A NEW PIT

Soon workers discover the earth walls of a fourth pit. It is empty. Why would the emperor's tomb builders prepare a chamber and then leave it empty? Perhaps they were interrupted before they could put anything in it. Ancient writings say that the tomb complex was still unfinished when Qin Shi Huangdi died suddenly in 210 B.C. One archaeologist suggests that the builders left the pit empty on purpose. Maybe its contents were supposed to be spiritual, not physical. This question needs more study.

Months pass. The exciting work in the pits continues. On many days, however, no one can work in the pits. Rainstorms fill the trenches with water and wash dirt back into the pits. The water reburies items that archaeologists spent weeks or months unearthing and cleaning. Bad weather is a real threat to these priceless objects. So is theft. Modern burglars try to carry off relics from the site. Guards must watch over the pits day and night.

It's clear to everyone that they must do something to protect the ancient army. They need a building—a museum—especially made to house the emperor's treasures.

This horse was found in Pit 2. It originally had both a bridle and a saddle. In order to preserve finds such as this horse, archaeologists filled Pit 2 and Pit 3 before the heavy rains came.

The Museum of Terra Cotta Warriors and Horses in Lintong County has become a huge
tourist attraction since its opening in October 1979. This is the entrance to Pit 1.

CHAPTER five

THE MUSEUM OF TERRA COTTA WARRIORS AND HORSES

It is a warm day in October 1979. A crowd of children moves quickly through the building's doors. They enter the newly opened Museum of Terra Cotta Warriors and Horses. Like most Chinese boys and girls, they have learned about Qin Shi Huangdi's clay army. They have followed newspaper accounts of the army's discovery with great interest. They chatter excitedly. They are amazed and delighted to see row after row of the warriors.

Archaeologists working in the pits below know exactly how the children feel. They must resist the temptation to look away from their work. Having people watching their every move is something new. Soon they will get used to the noise and movement overhead. But at this time, it is distracting and also quite exciting. The team has dreamed about sharing the terra cotta figures with the world. That dream is finally coming true.

The museum opening is an important event for everyone involved. Workers finished building a massive exhibition hall over Pit 1. The three-part museum contains an entry room, corridor, and exhibition hall. The building is 755 feet (230 m) long, 236 feet (72 m) wide, and 72 feet (22 m) high. With a total area of nearly 53,000 square feet (4,924 sq. m), it protects Pit 1 from weather and thieves.

THE WORK CONTINUES

Excavation work had stopped during the building of the museum. With the museum open, the dig can begin again.

The pit area is divided into twenty-seven separate sections. Much of this area is still unexplored. But soon the work of unearthing hidden treasures begins again.

The team working on the job includes dozens of students, laborers, and expert archaeologists. Yuan Zhongyi still leads the team. He is also the director of the new museum.

The interior of Pit 1 as it looks in the 2000s. Much more has been excavated since 1979, and a lot of work is yet to be done.

Weather and security are no longer problems. The archaeological teams can work all year-round. The museum also makes it possible for visitors to view the excavation close up. These visitors watch from raised wooden walkways around the pit.

Before the museum opened, dozens of reassembled terra cotta warriors stood in sheds near the site. But workers carefully return the statues to their original places in the pits. They wrap the heavy figures with cloth to protect them. Then, using hand-operated pulleys, they gently lower the soldiers back into place. Soon hundreds of warriors line the corridors of the pits. The soldiers stand in rows as they once did twenty-two hundred years ago.

Almost, at least. The excavated figures do not look exactly the way they did when they were buried in 210 B.C. The paint that once covered them is still flaking off. No one has been able to find a way to stop it. With no real solution to the paint problem, the team members worry about unearthing any more figures.

CHARIOTS

Some experts study the paint and do tests on it. Meanwhile, other teams focus on things that can be safely excavated. Among these are chariots and weapons. The chariots are some of the rarest discoveries at the Qin tomb site. No one has found anything like them in such huge numbers before. Of course, all the wooden parts of the chariots have rotted away. But experts have studied prints that the wood left in the soil. They have also examined many metal parts found near the imprints. The archaeologists use these clues to make exact models of these two-wheeled vehicles.

Archaeologists and other experts scurry to keep up with all these new developments. There is so much to study. Meanwhile, diggers continue to clear away soil and debris in Pit 1. The pit's incredible size is just becoming clear. It covers about 50,000 square feet (4,645 sq. m). By the end of 1979, workers have only excavated five sections on the eastern end. These sections make up less than one-fifth of Pit 1's entire area. Yuan says that it might take five years or more to finish excavating all twenty-seven sections of Pit 1. Pits 2 and 3, just to the north, remain filled in for safety.

Pit 1 is the largest of the three pits. It holds the most soldiers. Each soldier is unique in some way.

Eventually, they will be covered with buildings and fully excavated too.

In Pit 1, archaeologists have already discovered eight wooden chariots, thirty-two life-sized terra cotta horses, and more than one thousand warriors. Each warrior stands 5 feet 9 inches (175 centimeters) tall. In addition, workers have found more than ten thousand bronze weapons. They estimate that more than six thousand terra cotta soldiers and horses, dozens more war chariots, and tens of thousands of weapons exist in all.

Spellbound museum visitors watch as the archaeologists continue their work in the trenches. They kneel or bend down, concentrating carefully on half-buried figures. They barely touch the clay with their brushes, wooden picks, and small metal tools. Most wear white masks over their mouths and noses. The masks protect the workers, keeping them from breathing in tiny dust particles. And they may also protect the statues. Some scientists believe bacteria in workers' breath may actually harm the terra cotta. Until they know for sure, they must be careful.

"The most difficult part of the whole operation is sorting out the remains of the chariots and the hand weapons. Destroyed by fire and buried in the collapsed vaults, the wooden chariots have become utterly unrecognizable. Great pains have to be taken to set the unrelated shambles aside in order to have a clear view of what were once the wheels, the shafts or the bodies. Likewise the wooden shafts of the weapons and arrows are thoroughly decayed but, in some cases, their forms have been preserved in print marks, some even with the patterns of the feathers that have rotted away. These must not be touched with any degree of haste, but can only be sorted out with thin bamboo sticks and [tiny] brushes."

—Chinese author Yu Tien Wei, 1988

REBUILDING A FIGHTING FORCE

One of the many important things the terra cotta army tells us is how ancient armies were set up for battle. Many historians wrote about warfare tactics and techniques. But the terra cotta army is an example of what a real Chinese army looked like and how it fought. As workers place the figures in their original positions, an image of an ancient fighting force becomes clear for the first time.

The First Emperor's army in Pit 1, for instance, stands in a huge rectangle. One unit of about two hundred warriors faces east. Behind these warriors are middle ranks of several thousand soldiers. Most of these central units are infantry (soldiers who fight on foot), and they face east. A rear unit of about one hundred soldiers faces west. In addition, rows of archers on the outside face north and south. These soldiers hold bows and arrows. They are ready to protect the unit from attack from those directions.

Soldiers in the front unit wear no armor or helmets. They once carried crossbows and longbows. Longbows were wooden bows about 5 or 6 feet (1.5 to 1.8 m) long. The warriors of the large center unit do wear armor. They once carried spears, swords, and other long-shafted weapons. This main group stands in eleven long rows.

Several horse-pulled chariots are also part of the main battle unit. Each one once carried an armored driver and one or two warriors. These men also held spears or other weapons. The group of soldiers around each chariot probably cooperated with the chariot and its riders during battle.

Along with the infantry and chariots were units of cavalrymen. These expert horsemen could ride and shoot a crossbow at the same time. Workers have found more than 160 cavalrymen with horses in Pit 2. Each soldier stands in front of his animal, one hand clutching the horse's rein and the other clenched around a crossbow.

A TOUGH ARMY

Historians say that Qin horses were specially bred and trained for battle. They were the strongest, most spirited animals available. The horses of the terra cotta army have eager eyes, tense muscles, flared nostrils, and wide neighing mouths. Everything about the army presents a picture of organization and strength. They look totally unbeatable.

Looking this way was no accident. For an ancient army marching forward, appearing unstoppable was sometimes half the battle. In fact, old stories say that just the sight of Qin's vast army moving toward the battlefield was often enough to send enemies fleeing in terror.

But just looking powerful was not enough. The Qin army was more than ready to strike with incredible force. The many different weapons in the pits with the warriors show this. After studying these weapons, archaeologists have separated them into close-range and long-range weapons. Close-range weapons include swords, knives, spears, clubs, and axes. Warriors used them in hand-to-hand combat. Long-range weapons include longbows, crossbows, and bronze-tipped arrows.

These Qin weapons were the best of their day. The Qin crossbow is especially impressive. In its time, it was the most powerful weapon in the world. It had a range of nearly 2,700 feet (823 m). And its design made it faster to load and easier to shoot than older models. Qin factories mass-produced this improved crossbow.

Ancient Songs

The workers have found some musical instruments in the pits among the warriors and chariots. Ancient accounts tell us that the sounds of drums and bells told soldiers how and where to move in battle. Soldiers at the rear of the force or riding on chariots used these instruments to guide the army according to their officers' orders. The officers often watched the action from hilltops nearby. A single, regular drumbeat told the army to move steadily forward. A faster beat or drumroll meant "Attack!" The sound of a bell ordered warriors to stop. A repeated ringing signaled a retreat. Historians say that, directed by these signals, the Qin army operated like a giant machine. Each part acted in perfect harmony with the others.

This bronze bell was one of the musical instruments discovered in the pits.

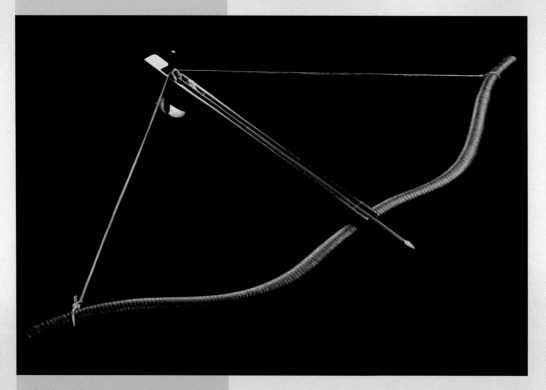

Archaeologists reconstructed this crossbow using a bronze trigger mechanism found at the terra cotta site. The bronze arrowhead was also found with the terra cotta army.

The pits also hold extralong arrows. Their tips are made of razor-sharp bronze. Workers find these arrows in bundles with other arrows. The archaeologists think that Qin archers used these arrows in crossbows. All of these excellent weapons gave the Qin army a big advantage in battle.

According to ancient lore, Qin soldiers charged into battle without armor or helmets. This gave them a reputation as wild and fearless. In addition, the legends say that not carrying extra weight made Qin warriors faster and more nimble than armored soldiers. The Qin army used this advantage well. They were a powerful and deadly fighting force.

The terra cotta figures prove that some of the ancient stories about the Qin army were true. They show that others were only partly true. For instance, most of the warriors in the front at Pit 1 wear no armor, just as the stories said. But most of the infantry, archers, and chariot drivers do. The teams have identified a total of seven different types of armor. Evidence in the pits shows that most soldiers wore leather armor. The

Qin Weapons

Workers have found three unusual weapons at the Qin site. They are the *pi*, *wandao*, and *shu*. The pi is a sickle-shaped, 1-foot-long (0.3 m) spearhead on the end of a 10-foot-long (3 m) pole. Ancient books mention the pi, but this is the first one the archaeologists have ever seen. The experts have also never seen a real wandao before. This curved sword is shaped like a crescent moon. The archaeologists think that this weapon already had a long tradition by the time of the Qin dynasty. The shu is a narrow, heavy piece of metal shaped like a cylinder. It is about 6 inches (15 cm) long and 1 inch (2.5 cm) across, with a pointed top. It was attached to the top of a long pole. Warriors riding in fast-moving chariots swung shu like clubs. Workers have found a bundle of these ancient defensive weapons in Pit 3. Some even have parts of their original wooden poles.

These weapons were discovered in Pit 2. They appear to be a store of crossbow arrows.

leather was coated with thick layers of lacquer. This coating was made from the sap of a tree that grows in China. It dried clear and made a shell as hard as rock. Other armor was made from overlapping plates of bronze, iron, or stone.

During his life, Emperor Qin set out to build the perfect fighting force. Stories of his army's victories show that he must have come close. It seems that the emperor did not want to take any chances, though. He also built a perfect terra cotta army to protect him after his death.

In 1980 workers at the terra cotta site discovered this bronze chariot and four horses in

CHAPTER six

CHARIOTS FOR
THE EMPEROR

In December 1980, workers near Qin's tomb make yet another amazing discovery. About 66 feet (20 m) west of the burial mound, test probes reveal something unusual. Test holes unearth a huge group of bronze pieces about 25 feet (8 m) below the ground. They are different from anything found so far.

Over the next several months, workers slowly unearth pieces of two beautiful bronze chariots. These chariots are about half the size of the others the team has found. They are broken into thousands of small parts. But expert eyes can see how they once looked. Finding them is like opening yet another new window into the past.

Four bronze horses once pulled each two-wheeled chariot. These horses were painted white. The hardware and fittings on the wagons and horses are mainly silver and gold. Delicate painted patterns decorate the precious metal.

Each chariot also has a bronze driver. Wide bronze umbrellas protect the drivers from sun and rain. The drivers' clothing and hairstyles tell experts that these men held very high ranks in the army.

The drivers are in amazingly good condition. So are several bronze servants. They hold swords, ready to guard each side of the chariots. All

This black-and-white photograph shows a bronze chariot with its driver and horses as it looked shortly after being discovered in the early 1980s.

together, this find appears to be a royal procession. Historians say that Emperor Qin loved such ceremonies.

The experts think that these chariots were for the emperor to use. Wu Yongqi, an archaeologist and director of the Museum of Terra Cotta Warriors and Horses, discusses this remarkable find. "If the terra cotta warriors were to protect the underground empire of the emperor as his army, the bronze chariots . . . were the vehicle for the journey of the emperor's soul."

NEW MYSTERIES

Pit 3 reopens in 1989. The pit is roughly shaped like an irregular letter *U*. It is much smaller than Pits 1 and 2. It is also different from the other pits in several ways. For instance, the inside of this chamber does not appear to have been burned. The other pits show evidence of raiders in ancient times setting the pits on fire.

Pit 3's overall purpose appears to be different as well. It was probably meant to serve as barracks and stables. Perhaps it's a place for the spirits of the emperor's best soldiers and horses to stay. A doorway on the east side of this chamber leads to what appears to have been a wooden stable. The stable once housed a war chariot and four terra cotta horses. A corridor to the right enters a large hall filled with warriors. The hall also contains the remains of a number of actual deer and other animals. These creatures appear to have been killed as part of some ritual or ceremony. Perhaps they were meant to be a meal for the warriors.

Other corridors also lead outward from the main room. These hallways hold sixty-eight soldiers. All of them are high-ranking officers. These warriors stand as if they are on guard duty. In addition, the figures in Pit 3 are taller. They are around 6 feet 2 inches (188 cm) tall, while those in the other pits stand 5 feet 9 inches (175 cm) high.

The archaeologists still think that Pit 3's main chamber represents a command center for a high-ranking person. Workers have not found a figure representing such a general or official. But the large ceremonial weapons the warriors once held were shu. In Qin times, warriors used them mainly for defensive purposes, not for attack. Such weapons would have been used to help protect an important person.

By the end of 1984, workers have restored 28 clay horses and 714 additional clay warriors. These figures are back in their original locations in Pits 1 and 2. By 1988 museum visitors can view 20 more chariots, around 1,000 warriors, and more than 10,000 bronze weapons in the three main excavation areas.

Work in the pit of the bronze chariots continues, as well. Clues in the soil show that the two chariots once stood in a wooden shed or barn. Some archaeologists call this building a large coffin. They use

> Based on what has been excavated so far it seems that the royal [tomb] of the first emperor had been modeled on the palaces he lived [in] during his lifetime. The underground [tomb] is a replica of the palaces that once stood on the ground."
>
> —Yuan Zhongyi, 1984

this name because the area looks like the ceremonial burial boxes that rich, important people used in ancient times. The building was once brightly painted and decorated like those burial structures. It contains objects, such as the chariots, that wealthy people wanted to take with them after they died.

But the building's wooden structure rotted away many years ago. Afterward, the weight of the earth above and around the smaller chariots crushed them into thousands of small pieces. The chariots and their drivers are little more than a heap of metallic bits. The archaeologists admit that putting them back together will be a huge job.

Experts soon begin the work. First, they number and record each piece. They carefully take note of its exact location in relation to all the others. Artists make hundreds of drawings. Chinese scientists and scholars prefer drawings to photographs. Photos can be fuzzy, and shadows in pictures sometimes hide important details. Photographs cannot show what is beneath or behind objects, either. A skilled artist, however, can make drawings that show an object from all sides and even what lies beneath it.

Bronze restorers study the condition of each metallic piece. Then they decide the best way to reconnect it with others. Many pieces are bent or flattened. The earth's great weight has pressed down on them for centuries. Workers have to re-form these pieces into their original shapes. Metalworking specialists help decide how to do this job. Experts also help polish and clean the metal. It is dusty and dirty. But, after being buried for twenty-two hundred years, it is still in remarkably good condition.

ROYAL TRANSPORTATION

More than two years of study and preparation have passed. Finally, the

Luxury in the Afterlife

Archaeologists call tomb figures and other buried items *mingqi*, or "spirit articles." People placed these items in ancient tombs to re-create a dead person's earthly life. Putting rare and valuable items in a tomb also showed a ruler's power and status. An emperor's ability to sacrifice valuable objects—not to mention the lives of thousands of tomb builders—showed people how important he was.

restorers begin assembling the chariots. One small piece at a time, they rebuild them by hand. Team leaders estimate that the entire job could take between five to eight years.

But it doesn't take long to see how amazing the chariots are. How, for instance, did ancient metalworkers make the paper-thin bronze umbrellas protecting the drivers? These metal canopies are less than .08 inch (0.2 cm) thick. How did they make the intricate tassel decorations on each horse? The tassels are even thinner than the canopy. These metal creations are incredibly precise. Yet artists made them without any modern tools or technology. Restorers also marvel that the methods used for making many of the chariots' original moving parts are still used by modern craftspeople. Before finding the bronze chariots, no one knew ancient craftsmen were so advanced.

It takes thirty restorers seven years to reconstruct and restore the two bronze chariots. The larger chariot weighs more than 2,600 pounds (1,179 kilograms). Meanwhile, archaeologists continue to work in the pit where they found the chariots.

This bronze chariot, with its umbrella and driver, shows incredible creativity. It was found near the grave of Emperor Qin in 1980.

A HOST OF SPIRITS

Archaeologists also find the ruins of elaborate buildings and temples all around the tomb area. In ancient times, living people brought food offerings and other gifts to these buildings. Workers also discover bronze and jade bowls and pots around the tomb complex. Visitors to the tomb once used these containers to prepare feasts for the dead emperor and his companions.

Not far away, the team finds other pits containing the skeletons of real horses. A number of life-sized terra cotta figures—different from any found in other pits—are with them. Are they horse grooms and workers? Many archaeologists think so, but no one knows for sure. Still, experts do learn

Li Bai

A great Chinese poet named Li Bai (sometimes written Li Po or Li Pai) lived in China more than nine centuries after Qin Shi Huangdi's death. As a child, he grew up hearing stories of the terrible emperor of Qin. Later, Li Bai wrote a poem about him. Part of that poem speaks of the emperor's conquest of the warring kingdoms. It also describes his legendary cruelty and hunger for power. The section below talks about the building of his tomb complex.

This decoration from a porcelain plate shows the poet Li Bai. The plate dates back to the Kangxi period (1662–1722) of the Qing dynasty.

The Emperor of Ch'in [Qin] destroyed
All other kingdoms around him;
So fierce was he that he could
draw his sword and kill even
the clouds in heaven. . . .
He stood looking down at the world;
then he seized 700,000
conscripts [forced laborers] to start work
under the shadow of Lishan [Mount Li]; . . .
Now all we know is that in a great coffin
Below the yellow earth is the dust
Of this great emperor.

something from the pit's mixture of real animals and terra cotta figures. They already know that in ancient China, when wealthy and important people died, their families and servants were sometimes buried alive along with them. But archaeologists had not known how long this custom lasted. Emperor Qin's tomb shows them that the old custom had changed slightly by the time the emperor died. Otherwise, real servants and grooms would have been buried along with the horses.

Of course, the emperor could easily have ordered the burial of his entire living army. So why didn't he? The answer seems to be that he needed his warriors alive more than he needed them dead.

It was very important to Qin Shi Huangdi that his sons and grandsons follow him as emperors. He wanted his family to rule for centuries to come. But the First Emperor knew that others wanted the throne for themselves. He had made many enemies during his short lifetime. Armed uprisings would erupt as soon as he was gone. He needed a living army to protect his children. He hoped they would make sure that the Qin dynasty continued.

But his craftsmen were skilled enough to create a perfectly good terra cotta army. And during the Qin dynasty, the Chinese believed that, in the afterlife, the image of a thing was as good as the real thing. So the First Emperor was able to leave his human army behind to guard his earthly empire. Meanwhile, he took his terra cotta warriors with him to the spirit world.

Spirit Guardians

Most of the team's experts agree that human eyes were never supposed to see the terra cotta army. Ancient people believed that models of things or people in burial chambers became real after the dead person entered into the spirit world. That must be why Emperor Qin's workers built and buried this huge army. It was meant to follow the emperor's spirit and protect him in the next world. If he really was a cruel and violent ruler, as history suggests, he probably made many enemies during his lifetime. Perhaps he felt he would need a lot of protection in the next one.

Visitors to the Museum of Terra Cotta Warriors and Horses enter three separate buildings to see each of the three main pits. Someday, visitors also may be able to visit the mausoleum of the emperor.

CHAPTER seven

WITHIN THE EMPEROR'S TOMB

Qin Shi Huangdi's tomb complex and its museum have become known as the Eighth Wonder of the World. And in 1987, the United Nations Educational, Scientific and Cultural Organization lists the tomb as a World Heritage Site. Thousands of people visit the Museum of Terra Cotta Warriors and Horses every year.

But visitors only see the beginning. Archaeologists agree that it could take fifty to one hundred years to uncover the whole area. It covers more than 2 million square feet (185,806 sq. m). And as teams explore each new section of the tomb, they uncover more startling discoveries. For example, workers find the remains of rare birds and exotic animals in coffins containing dishes of food. Terra cotta statues of the animals' keepers are nearby. An estimated three hundred to four hundred additional pits are thought to hold other animals and attendants. All of these figures are part of a huge city meant for the dead emperor's pleasure.

EVER EXPANDING

In 1999 teams discover a burial pit containing some of the most unusual terra cotta figures ever found. They appear to be acrobats or entertainers. They strike a wild array of poses—lifting, spinning, dancing, jumping, and other movements.

In July 2000, farmers digging near their village on the far western border of the spirit city unearth pieces of more terra cotta warriors. Archaeologists go to investigate this new site. It becomes the 180th and most distant pit yet found with the First Emperor's tomb. There, the archaeologists are surprised to discover more than twelve life-sized bronze cranes. These birds have great spiritual meaning in Chinese culture. They symbolize long life and immortality. Test digs at the new spot show that the area may once have been a large park, complete with flowing pools and beautiful bronze birds and animals.

Closer to the tomb, workers have found pits holding suits of stone armor. They also unearth ceremonial containers, such as jade bowls and a 467-pound (212 kg) bronze cauldron. Other luxury items, such as mirrors and jewelry, show that the emperor probably buried everything that he and his court might want or need after death.

The spirit city also holds a pit of strange terra cotta figures wearing hats and long robes. They stand with their hands crossed at their

This terra cotta entertainer is ready to perform. Archaeologists found this and other unique statues of entertainers modeled in various positions.

Workers carefully put together this suit of stone armor from thousands of pieces found by archaeologists at the terra cotta site.

waists. Are they government officials? Could they be a panel of wise men? Maybe they represent the emperor's advisers, standing by in case their good counsel is needed. Or are they horse breeders and trainers? These animal experts were some of ancient China's most respected people. Modern scholars are still trying to decide who these figures are.

RELICS AND REMAINS

Digging reveals actual human remains in the tomb, as well. Close to the pits of horses and grooms is a row of seventeen pits filled with human bones. Some of these graves also hold pieces of silk, as well as jade, gold, and silver objects. These items show that these real people were extremely important and wealthy during their lifetimes. They may have been the emperor's children, killed in the rebellion that followed his death. Some scholars believe they may have even asked to die so that they could go with the emperor on his spirit journey.

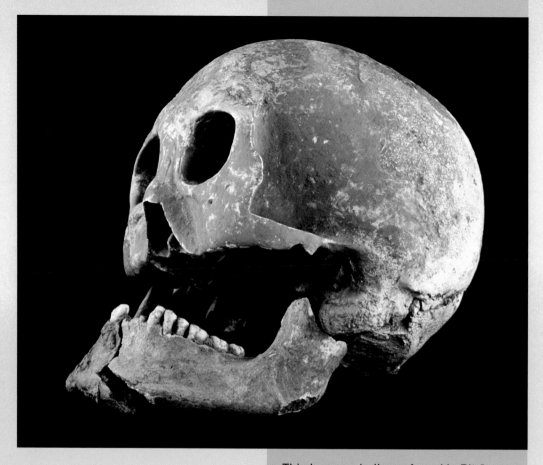

This human skull was found in Pit 2. Some archaeologists believe it belonged to a member of Qin Shi Huangdi's household. It may even have belonged to one of the emperor's sons. No one knows for certain.

That was not the case for more than one hundred other people. Workers find their remains in a mass grave about 1 mile (1.6 km) from the emperor's tomb. These people lie outside the spirit city. Clay tablets buried with the skeletons clearly identify them as forced laborers at the tomb complex. They had been sentenced to death for crimes. Because of these inscriptions, the archaeologists learn more about some of the Qin era's lowest-ranking people than they do about most of their noble superiors. Names, places of birth, and other information about these people are listed on the tablets. They are the oldest tomb inscriptions ever found in China. This discovery is important because it shows the contrast between these workers' hard lives and the luxurious lives of the people they served. One writer says that the terra cotta army is "art created in . . . suffering, a flash of talent generated in untold agony."

One strange new find is a terra cotta archer with a dark green face and black eyes. The team is not sure what this figure represents. Why did its ancient maker paint its face this way? The other eight thousand or so warriors discovered so far all have naturally colored faces. Only this one is green. Maybe it means that warriors sometimes painted their faces to frighten enemies. Or maybe it was a painter's error. No one knows for certain.

Another Army

Qin Shi Huangdi's terra cotta warriors are not the only buried army discovered in China. In 2003 workers found a tomb holding thousands of horses, chariots, and 1-foot-tall (0.3 m) terra cotta soldiers. This tomb lies south of Beijing. It dates from the Han dynasty (202 B.C-A.D. 220). This family ruled China after Qin.

Archaeologists are still studying new discoveries. But already experts believe that the practice of burying kings and nobles with symbolic armies must have been common in ancient China.

In 2003 workers found these terra cotta warriors south of Beijing. They date from the Han dynasty.

LOOKING TO THE FUTURE

Experts continue to study the vast number of objects already discovered. They also plan for more digging at the tomb complex. But as time passes, the main goal is preserving the entire site. One Chinese official has said, "The terra cotta army belongs to the whole world. We have . . . [a duty] to protect [it]."

In 2003 work begins on a historic park at the First Emperor's tomb site. This project aims to improve and secure the entire tomb complex area. The idea is to use modern techniques to save and protect what is there. At the same time, the project will make the site more open

This worker uses technology to monitor and test the air quality at the Museum of Terra Cotta Warriors and Horses. He and other workers use these tests to help protect the statues from pollutants, moisture, and the effects of changes in temperature.

A Dangerous New Enemy

More than two million people have visited the Museum of the Terra Cotta Warriors and Horses each year since 2000. But the crowds also bring billions more visitors that nobody wants. These uninvited guests are germs, mold, and mildew.

Bacteria of all kinds enter the site daily. Many arrive on food wrappers and paper cups from outside. Others come in on visitors' hands, clothing, and breath. These people lean over the railings to look at the figures every day. They do not mean to do harm. But the warm, damp terra cotta and surrounding earth make a perfect home for germs and molds.

Workers first notice a greenish, fuzzy-looking substance on some of the soldiers. Closer looks find similar growths on nearly all the figures and the surrounding earthen walls. Tests find that more than forty different kinds of bacteria are in the site.

Using a variety of modern tools, scientists from around the world have begun waging war against these tiny invaders. Their efforts seem to be working. It appears that the emperor's ancient army has won yet another battle.

to visitors and students. Planners hope to install a new subway system running to and from the site.

Team members also begin using computers more and more in their work. They use them to keep track of relics and to assist in reassembly and restoration. Computers also record temperature, humidity, and other information about pit conditions. And starting in 2005, Chinese and U.S. scientists work together on conserving paint and controlling pollution.

Some things are still beyond the reach of modern technology. Over the years, most people—both scientists and the public—keep asking one question. What lies beneath Qin Shi Huangdi's high burial mound? Modern science has ways of investigating this mystery. But so far, they have raised as many questions as they've answered. One thing is certain.

Something is definitely down there. Is the emperor's own tomb really as rich with jewels and gold as legends say? The only way to know for sure is to dig it up. But doing so could destroy the very things the world has been waiting to see for more than two thousand years. Yuan Zhongyi

Thousands of terra cotta soldiers stand in tightly packed rows to guard the tomb of Emperor Qin.

wants to be on the safe side. He says, "Until we can find the best way to protect [fragile artifacts], it's better to leave them in the ground." Wu Yongqi agrees. "Until our generation, or the next generation, figures out a good plan, it's best to just leave things alone."

The famous tenor Plácido Domingo played the title role of Emperor Qin Shi Huangdi in the Metropolitan Opera Company's *The First Emperor*. This opera opened in New York in 2006.

EPILOGUE

After more than thirty years, experts are just beginning to understand the full meaning of Qin Shi Huangdi's tomb. With each passing year, it is clearer that all parts of the complex are connected like the pieces of a puzzle. Each new discovery adds to the picture. The pieces show that the vast spirit city was a grand plan by Qin Shi Huangdi. The emperor and his advisers seem to have designed the complex so that he could enjoy the same luxuries after his death as he had in life.

Meanwhile, fascination with the First Emperor and his terra cotta army has grown too. Whether the emperor was a good or bad man seems to matter less than his exciting story. A flurry of books, movies, and computer games based on his life has appeared. The Metropolitan Opera Company in New York City has even produced an opera called *The First Emperor*.

History shows that Qin Shi Huangdi spent much of his life searching for the secret to eternal life. Apparently, he did not find it. Modern investigation shows that his tomb is, indeed, occupied. But the discovery of the First Emperor's amazing terra cotta army has made him famous around the world. His name lives on. That fame, in itself, is a kind of immortality.

MAP OF THE TERRA COTTA WARRIORS DISCOVERY SITE

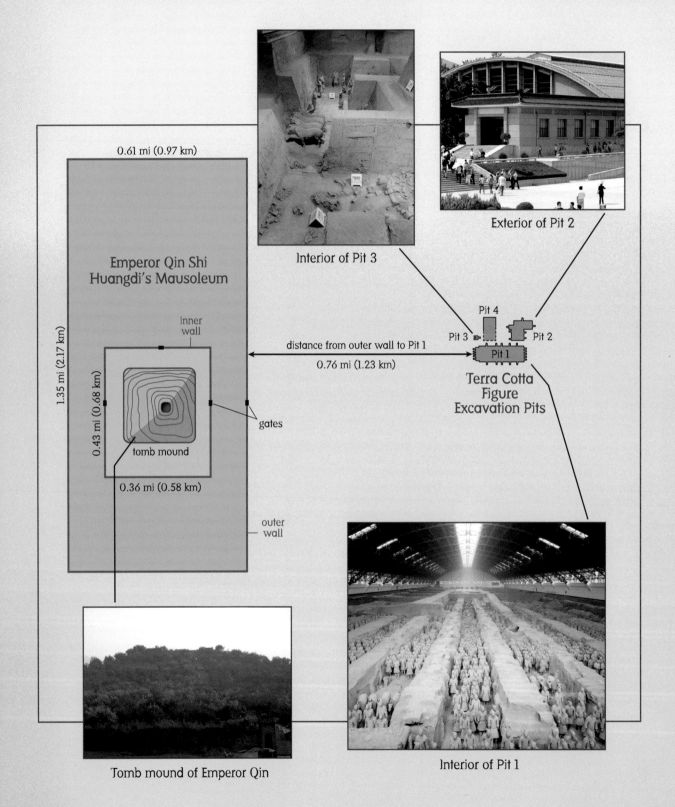

0.61 mi (0.97 km)

Emperor Qin Shi Huangdi's Mausoleum

inner wall

1.35 mi (2.17 km)

0.43 mi (0.68 km)

tomb mound

0.36 mi (0.58 km)

gates

outer wall

distance from outer wall to Pit 1
0.76 mi (1.23 km)

Pit 4

Pit 3

Pit 2

Pit 1

Terra Cotta
Figure
Excavation Pits

Interior of Pit 3

Exterior of Pit 2

Tomb mound of Emperor Qin

Interior of Pit 1

TIMELINE

259 B.C.
Prince Zheng, son of King Zhuangxiang of Qin, is born.

246 B.C.
King Zhuangxiang of Qin dies. Zheng becomes king of Qin at the age of thirteen.

221 B.C.
Qin's army defeats Qi, last of the main Warring States. King Zheng takes the title Qin Shi Huangdi (First Emperor).

219 B.C.
Qin Shi Huangdi makes the first tour of his new empire.

214 B.C.
Workers begin building the Great Wall.

210 B.C.
Qin Shi Huangdi dies suddenly. His son, Hu Hai, takes the throne as Er Shi Huangdi (Second Emperor).

209 B.C.
A revolt against the Qin dynasty begins.

207 B.C.
The Qin army is defeated. The Second Emperor and three hundred Qin family members are captured and killed.

206 B.C.
The rebel army takes the Qin capital, Xianyang. They loot and burn the First Emperor's palaces and tomb.

202 B.C.
General Liu Bang sets up the Han dynasty, which would last four hundred years.

A.D. 1961
The People's Republic of China makes Qin Shi Huangdi's burial mound one of China's important historical sites.

1962
Scientists begin studying the tomb mound.

1974
Farmers digging a well find the first terra cotta figures.

1976
Workers find Pits 2 and 3, containing more terra cotta warriors.

1979
The Museum of Terra Cotta Warriors and Horses opens to the public.

1980
Teams unearth two bronze chariots in Pit 2.

1991
A new and improved airport opens in Xi'an to receive visitors coming to see the terra cotta army.

1994
Builders finish structures over Pits 2 and 3.

1995
Workers discover Pit 4.

1999
Teams find a green-faced warrior, a bronze cauldron, and figures of acrobats and entertainers.

2000
Scientists begin test digs at the tomb mound. Forty types of mold and bacteria threaten the terra cotta army.

2001
Workers find thirteen bronze cranes, as well as a pit of terra cotta civilian officials. Paint preservation and restoration begins on terra cotta figures.

2002
Teams discover stables, birds, and rare animal figures. Experts identify thousands of pieces of bamboo found in a well in Hunan Province as official Qin documents.

2003
Shaanxi Province begins work on a historic park at the Qin tomb site.

2004
Scientists use new technology to examine the Mount Li burial mound.

2005

Workers find a large number of coins beneath the burial mound. U.S. and Chinese scientists launch a cooperative program to study the effects of indoor pollution on the terra cotta army.

2006

The Metropolitan Opera Company in New York City presents *The First Emperor*, an opera based on the emperor of Qin's life.

2007

Archaeologists discover another new chamber in the emperor's tomb complex.

PRONUNCIATION GUIDE

Most Chinese words and names in this book are written in Pinyin. Pinyin is the most common method of writing Chinese characters using the western, Latin alphabet. Some Chinese words in titles and quotations are written in an older form called Wade-Giles. In those cases, the Pinyin spelling is in parentheses next to the Wade-Giles word. Words using the Wade-Giles method are generally pronounced the way they appear to English speakers. Pinyin words are pronounced according to the general guidelines below.

LETTERS	PRONUNCIATION
ai	eye
c	ts
i	ee
ou	oh
ui	ay
q	ch
u	oo
ü	ew
x	sh
z	ds
zh	zhuh

Other letters are pronounced almost as they are in English. In addition, the different stresses on syllables in Chinese words are very slight. Here are the pronunciations of some of the Chinese words that appear in the text:

Er Shi Huangdi	ar sher hwong-dee
Hu Hai	hoo hi
Lintong	lin-tong
Qin	chin
Shaanxi	shahn-shee
Shi Huangdi	sher hwong-dee
Shiji	sher-jee
Sima Qian	suh-mah chee-en
Wei	way
Wu Yongqi	woo yung-chee
Xi'an	shee-ahn
Xianyang	shee-en-yahng
Yuan Zhongyi	yew-an jong-ee
Zheng	jung
Zhongguo	chung-kwoh
Zhuangxiang	zhoo-wong-shee-en

GLOSSARY

cauldron: a large metal container or pot

chariot: a two-wheeled vehicle pulled by horses. In ancient times, armies often used chariots in warfare. They were also used for transportation.

crossbow: a weapon made of a bow placed crossways on a wooden frame. The frame holds an arrow against the bow's string. A shooter pulls back the string and aims the crossbow like a rifle. A trigger releases the string, which shoots the arrow with great force.

dynasty: a line of kings or rulers from one family

Hu Hai: son of the First Emperor. After his father's death in 210 B.C., he was named Er Shi Huangdi, or the Second Emperor. He was killed in 208 B.C.

jade: a hard, pale green (or white) gemstone often carved into various shapes. Ancient peoples valued jade highly.

probe: a drill-like tool attached to a long pole. Archaeologists use this tool to take samples of soil beneath the ground's surface.

Qin: the name of an ancient kingdom in what is northwestern China in modern times. Pronounced *Chin*, the name is thought to be the basis of the name of the nation Qin Shi Huangdi unified in 221 B.C.

Shi Huangdi: the name taken by Zheng, king of Qin, in 221 B.C.

shu: a large ceremonial weapon. In ancient times, soldiers used shu mainly for defensive purposes, rather than for attack.

spirit city: a tomb complex built to resemble a city. Spirit cities were based on the belief in some cultures that, after death, the spirit lives on in much the same way the person did while alive.

terra cotta: a type of clay baked at high temperatures until it is hard and waterproof

Warring States: seven powerful kingdoms (Qin, Han, Wei, Zhao, Chu, Qi, and Yan) that in ancient times made up the area known in modern times as China. From 480 to 221 B.C., the states were at war with one another. The First Emperor ended the wars when he conquered the states and united them into one empire.

Zheng: the birth name of Qin Shi Huangdi

Zhongguo: meaning "the Central Kingdom," the name given in ancient times to the empire Qin Shi Huangdi formed. It was made up mostly of the conquered Warring States, and it makes up much of what is known as modern China.

Zhuangxiang: king of Qin (250–247 B.C.) and father of the First Emperor

WHO'S WHO?

Dr. Yuan Zhongyi was born in China's Tongshan County, in Jiangsu Province, in 1932. He first came to the Qin tomb site in July 1974. He was a working archaeologist and deputy director of the Shaanxi Provincial Archaeological Research Institute. At the time, Yuan thought his work would take only a week or two. He has been at the excavation, in one capacity or another, ever since. As the "chief excavator of the terra cotta army," Yuan has been involved in nearly every part of the work. When the new Museum of Terra Cotta Warriors and Horses opened in 1978, he became its director. He was the director until 1998, when Wu Yongqi took over the position. Since then Yuan has traveled all over the world speaking at conferences and giving lectures. He has personally greeted four U.S. presidents and many other world leaders at the site. He has also been in many films and news reports about the First Emperor's terra cotta army.

In a 1994 interview, Yuan talked about his work. "Of course, on the whole, archaeological work is quite demanding," he said. "But being an archaeologist has its great rewards. Every time you discover something new, you experience an unbelievable excitement. We are often in a very elated mood. And we really feel privileged. To have been personally involved with the discovery of one of the wonders of the world is to be very lucky. That was the most exciting and rewarding part of my professional life as an archaeologist."

Yuan no longer works daily in the tomb's trenches. But he still keeps a close eye on excavation. And he still gets excited with each remarkable new discovery at the Qin tomb complex.

SOURCE NOTES

10   Faison, Seith, "Two Tales of Who Found Terra Cotta Men," *New York Times International,* June 25, 1998, A9.

17   *The First Emperor of China*, interactive videodisc, multimedia CD, produced by Ching-chih Chen, sponsored by NEH. (New York: Voyager Company, 1994). Quotations used courtesy of Ching-chih Chen.

18   Ibid.

20   Lothar Ledderose, *Ten Thousand Things: Module and Mass Production in Chinese Art* (Princeton, NJ: Princeton University Press, 1997), 59. Quotation used courtesy of Lothar Ledderose.

21   *The First Emperor of China.*

23   Raymond Dawson, trans., *Historical Records, Sima Qina,* (New York: Oxford University Press, 1994.)

27   O. Louis Mazzatenta, "China's Warriors Rise from the Earth," *National Geographic*, 190 (October 1996): 82.

28   Lois Ember, "The Army of Clay of China's First Emperor Visits the U.S.," *Chemical Engineering News* 56 (November 29, 1999): 37.

39   T`ien-wei Yü, *The First Emperor's Terra Cotta Legion* (Beijing: China Travel and Tourism Press, 1988), 34.

Quotations used by permission of Yuan Zhongyi.

46   Catharina Blänsdorf, Erwin Emmerling, and Michael Petzet, *Qin Shi Huangdi: The Terra Cotta Army of the First Chinese Emperor* (Munich: Bayerisches Landesamt für Demkmalpflege, 2001), 317.

47   Archaeological Team of Pit of Terra-Cotta Figures at Qin Shi Huang Mausoleum and the Museum of Qin Terra-Cotta Figures, comp., *Terra-Cotta Warriors and Horses at the Tomb of Qin Shi Huang, the First Emperor of China* (Beijing: Cultural Relics Publishing House, 1987), 18–19.

50   Rewi Alley, trans., *Li Pai: 200 Selected Poems.* (Hong Kong: Joint Publishing Company, 1980), 112–13. Quotation used courtesy of Joint Publishing Company.

57   T`ien-wei Yü, 192.

58   Blänsdorf, Emmerling, and Petzet, 236.

61   Archaeological Team, 19.

61   Ibid.

SELECTED BIBLIOGRAPHY

Alley, Rewi, trans. *Li Pai: 200 Selected Poems*. Hong Kong: Joint Publishing Company, 1980.

Archaeological Team of Pit of Terra-Cotta Figures at Qin Shi Huang Mausoleum and the Museum of Qin Terra-Cotta Figures, comp. *Terra-Cotta Warriors and Horses at the Tomb of Qin Shi Huang, the First Emperor of China*. Beijing: Cultural Relics Publishing House, 1987, 1–21.

Blänsdorf, Catharina, Erwin Emmerling, and Michael Petzet. *Qin Shi Huangdi: The Terra Cotta Army of the First Chinese Emperor*. Munich: Bayerisches Landesamt für Demkmalpflege, 2001.

Cotterell, Arthur. *The First Emperor of China: The Greatest Archeological Find of Our Time*. New York: Holt, Rinehart, and Winston, 1981.

Dawson, Raymond, trans. *Historical Records, Sima Qian*. New York: Oxford University Press, 1994.

The First Emperor of China. Interactive videodisc, multimedia CD. Produced by Ching-chih Chen. Sponsored by NEH. New York: Voyager Company, 1994.

Forte, Maurizio, and Alberto Siliotti, eds. *Virtual Archaeology: Re-creating Ancient Worlds*. New York: Harry N. Abrams, 1997, 222–227.

Fu Tianchou. *Wonders from the Earth: The First Emperor's Underground Army*. San Francisco: China Books and Periodicals, 1989.

Hearn, Maxwell K. "The Chinese Army Rises from Underground Sentinel Duty," *Smithsonian* 10 (November 1979): 38–51.

Hessler, Peter. "Rising to Life." *National Geographic* 200 (October 2001): 48+.

Hoh, Erling. "China's Great Enigma: What's Inside the Unexcavated Tomb of Emperor Qin Shi Huangdi?" *Archaeology* 54 (September/October 2001): 34.

Kern, Martin. *The Stele Inscriptions Ch'in Shihuang: Text and Ritual in Early Chinese Imperial Representation*. New Haven, CT: American Oriental Society, 2000.

Kesner, Ladislov. "Likeness of No One: (Re)presenting the First Emperor's Army," *Art Bulletin* 77 (March 1995): 115–132.

Ledderose, Lothar. *Ten Thousand Things: Module and Mass Production in Chinese Art*. Princeton, NJ: Princeton University Press, 1997.

Lindesay, William. *The Terra Cotta Army of the First Emperor of China*. Hong Kong: Odyssey Books and Guides, 1998.

Mazzatenta, O. Louis. "China's Warriors Rise from the Earth." *National Geographic* 190 (October 1996): 68–85.

Nesnick, Victoria C. "Secrets of the Tomb," *National Geographic World* 289 (September 1999): 25–30.

Nienhauser, William H., Jr., ed. *The Grand Scribe's Records, the Basic Annals of Pre-Han China by Ssu-ma Ch'ien*. Translated by Tsai-fa Cheng. Vol. 1. Bloomington: University of Indiana Press, 1994.

Rudolph, Richard C. "Archaeology News—The First Emperor's Underground Army: An Important Chinese Find." *Archaeology* 28 (October 1975): 267–269.

Topping, Audrey. "China's Army of the Dead." *Science Digest* 90 (February 1982): 72–75, 95.

———. "Clay Soldiers: The Army of Emperor Chin." *Horizon* 19 (January 1977): 4–13.

———. "The First Emperor's Army: China's Incredible Find." *National Geographic* 153 (April 1978): 440–59.

Yü, T`ien-wei. *The First Emperor's Terra Cotta Legion*. Beijing: China Travel and Tourism Press, 1988.

FURTHER READING AND WEBSITES

BOOKS AND MAGAZINES

Behnke, Alison. *China in Pictures*. Minneapolis: Twenty-First Century Books, 2003.

Calliope Magazine. "China's First Emperor: Shi Huangdi." Special issue. (October 1997).

Dean, Arlan. *Terra-Cotta Soldiers: Army of Stone*. New York: Children's Press, 2005.

George, Charles. *The Clay Soldiers of China*. Detroit: KidHaven Press, 2006.

O'Conner, Jane. *The Emperor's Silent Army: Terra Cotta Warriors of Ancient China*. New York: Viking Press, 2002.

Patent, Dorothy Hinshaw. *The Incredible Story of China's Buried Warriors*. New York: Benchmark Books, 2000.

Sherman, Josepha. *Your Travel Guide to Ancient China*. Minneapolis: Twenty-First Century Books, 2004.

Woods, Michael, and Mary B. Woods. *Ancient Warfare: From Clubs to Catapults*. Minneapolis: Twenty-First Century Books, 2000.

WEBSITES

Mausoleum of the First Qin Emperor: World Heritage
http://whc.unesco.org/en/list/441
This site from the United Nations offers a map of the region and a short video about the army. It also provides information about other World Heritage sites.

Museum of Qin Terra Cotta Warriors and Horses
http://www.travelchinaguide.com/attraction/shaanxi/xian/terra_cotta_army/
This travel website highlights the museum and its displays, and includes many pictures as well as background information.

Rising to Life: Treasures of Ancient China
http://www7.nationalgeographic.com/ngm/data/2001/10/01/html/ft_200110 01.3.html
This National Geographic page presents an overview of the army, as well as several up-close images of individual soldiers and other finds.

WHTour—Terracotta Army
http://www.world-heritage-tour.org/asia/cn/terracotta/army.html
Take a virtual tour of Pit 1 at this UNESCO-run website.

INDEX

PHOTO ACKNOWLEDGMENTS

The images in this book are used with the permission of: © Keren Su/ China Span/Alamy, p. 4; The Art Archive/British Library, p. 6; © Laura Westlund/Independent Picture Service, pp. 7, 19, 64 (diagram); © Topham/ The Image Works, p. 8; © REUTERS/Andrew Wong, p. 9; © Lowell Georgia/CORBIS, p. 10; © Liu Liqun/ChinaStock, p. 11; © Holton Collection/SuperStock, p. 12; AP Photo, pp. 15, 46; © O. Louis Mazzatenta/ National Geographic Society Image Collection, pp. 17, 42; © DAROLLE RAYMOND/CORBIS SYGMA, p. 18; © John W. Banagan/Photographer's Choice/Getty Images, p. 21; Photo provided by TravelChinaGuide.com, p. 22; © Jerry Alexander/Stone/Getty Images, p. 24; AP Photo/Wang Yebiao, Xinhua, p. 26 (left); © Wolfgang Kaehler/CORBIS, p. 26 (right); © Richard Melloul/Sygma/CORBIS, p. 29; © akg-images/Laurent Lecat, pp. 30, 33; The Art Archive/Dagli Orti, p. 32; © Lee Snider/The Image Works, pp. 34, 64 (top right); © Tina Manley/History/Alamy, pp. 36, 43; AP Photo/Sergey Ponomarev, p. 38; © Asian Art & Archaeology, Inc./ CORBIS, p. 41; © akg-images, pp. 44, 49; The Art Archive/Musée Guimet Paris/Gianni Dagli Orti, p. 50; © Jose Fuste Raga/CORBIS, p. 52; © Scuderie del Quirinale Museum/Getty Images, p. 54; © FREDERIC J. BROWN/AFP/Getty Images, p. 55; © O. Louis Mazzatenta/National Geographic/Getty Images, pp. 56, 60–61; © STR/AFP/Getty Images, p. 57; © China Photos/Getty Images, p. 58; © TIMOTHY A. CLARY/AFP/Getty Images, p. 62; © Richard Nowitz/National Geographic/Getty Images, p. 64 (top left); © Keren Su/CORBIS, p. 64 (bottom left); © Martin Puddy/Asia Images/Getty Images, p. 64 (bottom right).

Front Cover: © Miguel Menéndez V./epa/CORBIS.

ABOUT THE AUTHOR

Michael Capek is the author of numerous stories, articles, and books for young readers, including *Artistic Trickery, Murals, A Ticket to Jamaica,* and *A Personal Tour of Shaker Village,* all published by Lerner Publishing Group. He is a retired English teacher and a native Kentuckian. His fascination with the terra cotta army began the moment he first saw some of the warriors in a museum exhibition in 1998.